THE ELEMENTS OF STYLE

THE ELEMENTS OF STYLE

WILLIAM STRUNK, JR.

W L C

THE ELEMENTS OF STYLE

I.

Introductory

This book is intended for use in English courses in which the practice of composition is combined with the study of literature. It aims to give in brief space the principal requirements of plain English style. It aims to lighten the task of instructor and student by concentrating attention (in Chapters II and III) on a few essentials, the rules of usage and principles of composition most commonly violated. The numbers of the sections may be used as references in correcting manuscript.

The book covers only a small portion of the field of English style, but the experience of its writer has been that once past the essentials, students profit most by individual instruction based on the problems of their own work, and that each instructor has his own body of theory, which he prefers to that offered by any textbook.

The writer's colleagues in the Department of English in Cornell University have greatly helped him in the preparation of his manuscript. Mr. George McLane Wood has kindly consented to the inclusion under Rule 11 of some material from his Suggestions to Authors.

The following books are recommended for reference or further study: in connection with Chapters II and IV, F. Howard Collins, *Author and Printer* (Henry Frowde); Chicago University Press, *Manual of Style*; T. L. De Vinne, *Correct Composition* (The Century Company); Horace Hart, *Rules for Compositors and Printers* (Oxford University Press); George McLane Wood, *Extracts from the Style-Book of the Government Printing Office* (United States Geological Survey); in connection with Chapters III and V, Sir Arthur Quiller-Couch, *The Art of Writing* (Putnams), especially the chapter, *Interlude on Jargon*; George McLane Wood, *Suggestions to Authors* (United States Geological Survey); John Leslie Hall, *English Usage* (Scott, Foresman and Co.); James P. Kelly, *Workmanship in Words* (Little, Brown and Co.).

It is an old observation that the best writers sometimes disregard the rules of rhetoric. When they do so, however, the reader will usually find in the sentence some compensating merit, attained at the cost of the violation. Unless he is certain of doing as well, he will probably do best to follow the rules. After he has learned, by their guidance, to write plain English adequate for everyday uses, let him look, for the secrets of style, to the study of the masters of literature.

II.

Elementary Rules of Usage

1. Form the possessive singular of nouns with 's.

Follow this rule whatever the final consonant. Thus write,

    Charles's friend
    Burns's poems
    the witch's malice

This is the usage of the United States Government Printing Office and of the Oxford University Press.

Exceptions are the possessives of ancient proper names in -es and -is, the possessive Jesus', and such forms as for conscience' sake, for righteousness' sake. But such forms as Achilles' heel, Moses' laws, Isis' temple are commonly replaced by

    the heel of Achilles
    the laws of Moses
    the temple of Isis

The pronominal possessives hers, its, theirs, yours, and oneself have no apostrophe.

2. In a series of three or more terms with a single conjunction, use a comma after each term except the last.

Thus write,

    red, white, and blue
    honest, energetic, but headstrong
    He opened the letter, read it, and made a note of its contents.

This is also the usage of the Government Printing Office and of the Oxford University Press.

In the names of business firms the last comma is omitted, as

    Brown, Shipley and Company

The abbreviation *etc.*, even if only a single term comes before it, is always preceded by a comma.

3. Enclose parenthetic expressions between commas.

The best way to see a country, unless you are pressed for time, is to travel on foot.

This rule is difficult to apply; it is frequently hard to decide whether a single word, such as *however*, or a brief phrase, is or is not parenthetic. If the interruption to the flow of the sentence is but slight, the writer may safely omit the commas. But whether the interruption be slight or considerable, he must never omit one comma and leave the other. Such punctuation as

Marjorie's husband, Colonel Nelson paid us a visit yesterday,

or

My brother you will be pleased to hear, is now in perfect health,

is indefensible.

Non-restrictive relative clauses are, in accordance with this rule, set off by commas.

The audience, which had at first been indifferent, became more and more interested.

Similar clauses introduced by where and when are similarly punctuated.

In 1769, when Napoleon was born, Corsica had but recently been acquired by France.

Nether Stowey, where Coleridge wrote *The Rime of the Ancient Mariner*, is a few miles from Bridgewater.

In these sentences the clauses introduced by which, when, and where are non-restrictive; they do not limit the application of the words on which they depend, but add, parenthetically, statements supplementing those in the principal clauses. Each sentence is a combination of two statements which might have been made independently.

> The audience was at first indifferent. Later it became more and more interested.

> Napoleon was born in 1769. At that time Corsica had but recently been acquired by France.

> Coleridge wrote *The Rime of the Ancient Mariner* at Nether Stowey. Nether Stowey is only a few miles from Bridgewater.

Restrictive relative clauses are not set off by commas.

> The candidate who best meets these requirements will obtain the place.

In this sentence the relative clause restricts the application of the word candidate to a single person. Unlike those above, the sentence cannot be split into two independent statements.

The abbreviations *etc.* and jr. are always preceded by a comma, and except at the end of a sentence, followed by one.

Similar in principle to the enclosing of parenthetic expressions between commas is the setting off by commas of phrases or dependent clauses preceding or following the main clause of a sentence. The sentences quoted in this section and under Rules 4, 5, 6, 7, 16, and 18 should afford sufficient guidance.

If a parenthetic expression is preceded by a conjunction, place the first comma before the conjunction, not after it.

> He saw us coming, and unaware that we had learned of his treachery, greeted us with a smile.

4. Place a comma before and or but introducing an independent clause.

> The early records of the city have disappeared, and the story of its first years can no longer be reconstructed.

> The situation is perilous, but there is still one chance of escape.

Sentences of this type, isolated from their context, may seem to be in need of rewriting. As they make complete sense when the comma is reached, the second clause has the appearance of an after-thought. Further, and, is the least specific of connectives.

Used between independent clauses, it indicates only that a relation exists between them without defining that relation. In the example above, the relation is that of cause and result. The two sentences might be rewritten:

> As the early records of the city have disappeared, the story of its first years can no longer be reconstructed.

> Although the situation is perilous, there is still one chance of escape.

Or the subordinate clauses might be replaced by phrases:

> Owing to the disappearance of the early records of the city, the story of its first years can no longer be reconstructed.

> In this perilous situation, there is still one chance of escape.

But a writer may err by making his sentences too uniformly compact and periodic, and an occasional loose sentence prevents the style from becoming too formal and gives the reader a certain relief. Consequently, loose sentences of the type first quoted are common in easy, unstudied writing. But a writer should be careful not to construct too many of his sentences after this pattern (see Rule 14).

Two-part sentences of which the second member is introduced by as (in the sense of because), for, or, nor, and while (in the sense of and at the same time) likewise require a comma before the conjunction.

If a dependent clause, or an introductory phrase requiring to be set off by a comma, precedes the second independent clause, no comma is needed after the conjunction.

> The situation is perilous, but if we are prepared to act promptly, there is still one chance of escape.

For two-part sentences connected by an adverb, see the next section.

5. *Do not join independent clauses by a comma.*

If two or more clauses, grammatically complete and not joined by a conjunction, are to form a single compound sentence, the proper mark of punctuation is a semicolon.

> Stevenson's romances are entertaining; they are full of exciting adventures.

> It is nearly half past five; we cannot reach town before dark.

It is of course equally correct to write the above as two sentences each, replacing the semicolons by periods.

> Stevenson's romances are entertaining. They are full of exciting adventures.

> It is nearly half past five. We cannot reach town before dark.

If a conjunction is inserted, the proper mark is a comma (Rule 4).

> Stevenson's romances are entertaining, for they are full of exciting adventures.

> It is nearly half past five, and we cannot reach town before dark.

Note that if the second clause is preceded by an adverb, such as accordingly, besides, so, then, therefore, or thus, and not by a conjunction, the semicolon is still required.

> I had never been in the place before; so I had difficulty in finding my way about.

In general, however, it is best, in writing, to avoid using so in this manner; there is danger that the writer who uses it at all may use it too often. A simple correction, usually serviceable, is to omit the word so, and begin the first clause with as:

> As I had never been in the place before, I had difficulty in finding my way about.

If the clauses are very short, and are alike in form, a comma is usually permissible:

Man proposes, God disposes.

The gate swung apart, the bridge fell, the portcullis was drawn up.

6. *Do not break sentences in two.*

In other words, do not use periods for commas.

> I met them on a Cunard liner several years ago. Coming home from Liverpool to New York.

> He was an interesting talker. A man who had traveled all over the world, and lived in half a dozen countries.

In both these examples, the first period should be replaced by a comma, and the following word begun with a small letter.

It is permissible to make an emphatic word or expression serve the purpose of a sentence and to punctuate it accordingly:

> Again and again he called out. No reply.

The writer must, however, be certain that the emphasis is warranted, and that he will not be suspected of a mere blunder in punctuation.

Rules 3, 4, 5, and 6 cover the most important principles in the punctuation of ordinary sentences; they should be so thoroughly mastered that their application becomes second nature.

7. A participial phrase at the beginning of a sentence must refer to the grammatical subject.

> Walking slowly down the road, he saw a woman accompanied by two children.

The word walking refers to the subject of the sentence, not to the woman. If the writer wishes to make it refer to the woman, he must recast the sentence:

> He saw a woman, accompanied by two children, walking slowly down the road.

Participial phrases preceded by a conjunction or by a preposition, nouns in apposition, adjectives, and adjective phrases come under the same rule if they begin the sentence.

> On arriving in Chicago, his friends met him at the station.
>
> When he arrived (or, On his arrival) in Chicago, his friends met him at the station.

———

> A soldier of proved valor, they entrusted him with the defence of the city.
>
> A soldier of proved valor, he was entrusted with the defence of the city.

———

> Young and inexperienced, the task seemed easy to me.
>
> Young and inexperienced, I thought the task easy.

———

> Without a friend to counsel him, the temptation proved irresistible.
>
> Without a friend to counsel him, he found the temptation irresistible.

———

Sentences violating this rule are often ludicrous.

> Being in a dilapidated condition, I was able to buy the house very cheap.

8. Divide words at line-ends, in accordance with their formation and pronunciation.

If there is room at the end of a line for one or more syllables of a word, but not for the whole word, divide the word, unless this involves cutting off only a single letter, or cutting off only two letters of a long word. No hard and fast rule for all words can be laid down. The principles most frequently applicable are:

a. Divide the word according to its formation:

know-ledge (not knowl-edge);

Shake-speare (not Shakes-peare);

de-scribe (not des-cribe);

atmo-sphere (not atmos-phere);

b. Divide "on the vowel:"

edi-ble (not ed-ible)

propo-sition

ordi-nary

espe-cial

reli-gious

oppo-nents

regu-lar

classi-fi-ca-tion (three divisions possible)

deco-rative

presi-dent

c. Divide between double letters, unless they come at the end of the simple form of the word:

Apen-nines

Cincin-nati

refer-ring

tell-ing.

The treatment of consonants in combination is best shown from examples:

for-tune

pic-ture

presump-tuous

illus-tration

sub-stan-tial (either division)

indus-try

instruc-tion

sug-ges-tion

incen-diary.

The student will do well to examine the syllable-division in a number of pages of any carefully printed book.

III.

Elementary Principles of Composition

9. Make the paragraph the unit of composition: one paragraph to each topic.

If the subject on which you are writing is of slight extent, or if you intend to treat it very briefly, there may be no need of subdividing it into topics. Thus a brief description, a brief summary of a literary work, a brief account of a single incident, a narrative merely outlining an action, the setting forth of a single idea, any one of these is best written in a single paragraph. After the paragraph has been written, it should be examined to see whether subdivision will not improve it.

Ordinarily, however, a subject requires subdivision into topics, each of which should be made the subject of a paragraph. The object of treating each topic in a paragraph by itself is, of course, to aid the reader. The beginning of each paragraph is a signal to him that a new step in the development of the subject has been reached.

The extent of subdivision will vary with the length of the composition. For example, a short notice of a book or poem might consist of a single paragraph. One slightly longer might consist of two paragraphs:

    A. Account of the work.

    B. Critical discussion.

A report on a poem, written for a class in literature, might consist of seven paragraphs:

    A. Facts of composition and publication.

    B. Kind of poem; metrical form.

    C. Subject.

    D. Treatment of subject.

E. For what chiefly remarkable.

F. Wherein characteristic of the writer.

G. Relationship to other works.

The contents of paragraphs C and D would vary with the poem. Usually, paragraph C would indicate the actual or imagined circumstances of the poem (the situation), if these call for explanation, and would then state the subject and outline its development. If the poem is a narrative in the third person throughout, paragraph C need contain no more than a concise summary of the action. Paragraph D would indicate the leading ideas and show how they are made prominent, or would indicate what points in the narrative are chiefly emphasized.

A novel might be discussed under the heads:

A. Setting.

B. Plot.

C. Characters.

D. Purpose.

A historical event might be discussed under the heads:

A. What led up to the event.

B. Account of the event.

C. What the event led up to.

In treating either of these last two subjects, the writer would probably find it necessary to subdivide one or more of the topics here given.

As a rule, single sentences should not be written or printed as paragraphs. An exception may be made of sentences of transition, indicating the relation between the parts of an exposition or argument.

In dialogue, each speech, even if only a single word, is a paragraph by itself; that is, a new paragraph begins with each change of speaker. The application of this rule, when dialogue and narrative are combined, is best learned from examples in well-printed works of fiction.

10. As a rule, begin each paragraph with a topic sentence; end it in conformity with the beginning.

Again, the object is to aid the reader. The practice here recommended enables him to discover the purpose of each paragraph as he begins to read it, and to retain the purpose in mind as he ends it. For this reason, the most generally useful kind of paragraph, particularly in exposition and argument, is that in which

a. the topic sentence comes at or near the beginning;

b. the succeeding sentences explain or establish or develop the statement made in the topic sentence; and

c. the final sentence either emphasizes the thought of the topic sentence or states some important consequence.

Ending with a digression, or with an unimportant detail, is particularly to be avoided.

If the paragraph forms part of a larger composition, its relation to what precedes, or its function as a part of the whole, may need to be expressed. This can sometimes be done by a mere word or phrase (again; therefore; for the same reason) in the topic sentence. Sometimes, however, it is expedient to precede the topic sentence by one or more sentences of introduction or transition. If more than one such sentence is required, it is generally better to set apart the transitional sentences as a separate paragraph.

According to the writer's purpose, he may, as indicated above, relate the body of the paragraph to the topic sentence in one or more of several different ways. He may make the meaning of the topic sentence clearer by restating it in other forms, by defining its terms, by denying the converse, by giving illustrations or specific instances; he may establish it by proofs; or he may develop it by showing its implications and consequences. In a long paragraph, he may carry out several of these processes.

1 Now, to be properly enjoyed, a walking tour should be gone upon alone.
(Topic sentence.)

2 If you go in a company, or even in pairs, it is no longer a walking tour in anything but name; it is something else and more in the nature of a picnic.
(The meaning made clearer by denial of the contrary.)

3 A walking tour should be gone upon alone, because freedom is of the essence; because you should be able to stop and go on, and follow this way or that, as the freak takes you; and because you must have your own pace, and neither trot alongside a champion walker, nor mince in time with a girl.
(The topic sentence repeated, in abridged form, and supported by three reasons; the meaning of the third ("you must have your own pace") made clearer by denying the converse.)

4 And you must be open to all impressions and let your thoughts take colour from what you see.
(A fourth reason, stated in two forms.)

5 You should be as a pipe for any wind to play upon.
(The same reason, stated in still another form.)

6 "I cannot see the wit," says Hazlitt, "of walking and talking at the same time.

7 When I am in the country, I wish to vegetate like the country," which is the gist of all that can be said upon the matter.
(6-7 the same reason as stated by Hazlitt.)

8 There should be no cackle of voices at your elbow, to jar on the meditative silence of the morning.
(Repetition, in paraphrase, of the quotation from Hazlitt.)

9 And so long as a man is reasoning he cannot surrender himself to that fine intoxication that comes of much motion in the open air, that begins in a sort of dazzle and sluggishness of the brain, and ends in a peace that passes comprehension.—Stevenson, Walking Tours.
(Final statement of the fourth reason, in language amplified and heightened to form a strong conclusion.)

---

1 It was chiefly in the eighteenth century that a very different conception of history grew up.
(Topic sentence.)

2 Historians then came to believe that their task was not so much to paint a picture as to solve a problem; to explain or illustrate the successive phases of national growth, prosperity, and adversity.
(The meaning of the topic sentence made clearer; the new conception of history defined.)

3 The history of morals, of industry, of intellect, and of art; the changes that take place in manners or beliefs; the dominant ideas that prevailed in successive periods; the rise, fall, and modification of political constitutions; in a word, all the conditions of national well-being became the subjects of their works.
(The definition expanded.)

4 They sought rather to write a history of peoples than a history of kings.
(The definition explained by contrast.)

5 They looked especially in history for the chain of causes and effects.
(The definition supplemented: another element in the new conception of history.)

6 They undertook to study in the past the physiology of nations, and hoped by applying the experimental method on a large scale to deduce some lessons of real value about the conditions on which the welfare of society mainly depend.—Lecky, The Political Value of History.
(Conclusion: an important consequence of the new conception of history.)

In narration and description the paragraph sometimes begins with a concise, comprehensive statement serving to hold together the details that follow.

The breeze served us admirably.

The campaign opened with a series of reverses.

The next ten or twelve pages were filled with a curious set of entries.

But this device, if too often used, would become a mannerism. More commonly the opening sentence simply indicates by its subject with what the paragraph is to be principally concerned.

> At length I thought I might return towards the stockade.

> He picked up the heavy lamp from the table and began to explore.

> Another flight of steps, and they emerged on the roof.

The brief paragraphs of animated narrative, however, are often without even this semblance of a topic sentence. The break between them serves the purpose of a rhetorical pause, throwing into prominence some detail of the action.

11. Use the active voice.

The active voice is usually more direct and vigorous than the passive:

> I shall always remember my first visit to Boston.

This is much better than

> My first visit to Boston will always be remembered by me.

The latter sentence is less direct, less bold, and less concise. If the writer tries to make it more concise by omitting "by me,"

> My first visit to Boston will always be remembered,

it becomes indefinite: is it the writer, or some person undisclosed, or the world at large, that will always remember this visit?

This rule does not, of course, mean that the writer should entirely discard the passive voice, which is frequently convenient and sometimes necessary.

> The dramatists of the Restoration are little esteemed today.

> Modern readers have little esteem for the dramatists of the Restoration.

The first would be the right form in a paragraph on the dramatists of the Restoration; the second, in a paragraph on the tastes of modern readers. The need of making a particular word the subject of the sentence will often, as in these examples, determine which voice is to be used.

The habitual use of the active voice, however, makes for forcible writing. This is true not only in narrative principally concerned with action, but in writing of any kind. Many a tame sentence of description or exposition can be made lively and emphatic by substituting a transitive in the active voice for some such perfunctory expression as there is, or could be heard.

There were a great number of dead leaves lying on the ground.

Dead leaves covered the ground.

The sound of the falls could still be heard.

The sound of the falls still reached our ears.

The reason that he left college was that his health became impaired.

Failing health compelled him to leave college.

It was not long before he was very sorry that he had said what he had.

He soon repented his words.

As a rule, avoid making one passive depend directly upon another.

Gold was not allowed to be exported.

It was forbidden to export gold (The export of gold was prohibited).

_____

He has been proved to have been seen entering the building.

It has been proved that he was seen to enter the building.

_____

In both the examples above, before correction, the word properly related to the second passive is made the subject of the first.

A common fault is to use as the subject of a passive construction a noun which expresses the entire action, leaving to the verb no function beyond that of completing the sentence.

_____

A survey of this region was made in 1900.
This region was surveyed in 1900.

_____

Mobilization of the army was rapidly carried out.

The army was rapidly mobilized.

_____

Confirmation of these reports cannot be obtained.

These reports cannot be confirmed.

_____

Compare the sentence, "The export of gold was prohibited," in which the predicate "was prohibited" expresses something not implied in "export."

12. Put statements in positive form.

Make definite assertions. Avoid tame, colorless, hesitating, non-committal language. Use the word not as a means of denial or in antithesis, never as a means of evasion.

He was not very often on time.

He usually came late.

He did not think that studying Latin was much use.

He thought the study of Latin useless.

The Taming of the Shrew is rather weak in spots. Shakespeare does not portray Katharine as a very admirable character, nor does Bianca remain long in memory as an important character in Shakespeare's works.   The women in The Taming of the Shrew are unattractive. Katharine is disagreeable, Bianca insignificant.

The last example, before correction, is indefinite as well as negative. The corrected version, consequently, is simply a guess at the writer's intention.

All three examples show the weakness inherent in the word not. Consciously or unconsciously, the reader is dissatisfied with being told only what is not; he wishes to be told what is. Hence, as a rule, it is better to express a negative in positive form.

not honest = dishonest

not important = trifling

did not remember = forgot

did not pay any attention to = ignored

did not have much confidence in = distrusted

The antithesis of negative and positive is strong:

Not charity, but simple justice.

Not that I loved Caesar less, but Rome the more.

Negative words other than not are usually strong:

The sun never sets upon the British flag.

13. Omit needless words.

Vigorous writing is concise. A sentence should contain no unnecessary words, a paragraph no unnecessary sentences, for the same reason that a drawing should have no unnecessary lines and a machine no unnecessary parts. This requires not that the writer make all his sentences short, or that he avoid all detail and treat his subjects only in outline, but that every word tell.

Many expressions in common use violate this principle:

the question as to whether	whether (the question whether)
there is no doubt but that	no doubt (doubtless)
used for fuel purposes	used for fuel
he is a man who	he
in a hasty manner	hastily
this is a subject which	this subject
His story is a strange one.	His story is strange.

In especial the expression the fact that should be revised out of every sentence in which it occurs.

owing to the fact that	since (because)
in spite of the fact that	though (although)
call your attention to the fact that	remind you (notify you)
I was unaware of the fact that	I was unaware that (did not know)
the fact that he had not succeeded	his failure
the fact that I had arrived	my arrival

See also under *case, character, nature, system* in Chapter V.

Who is, which was, and the like are often superfluous.

His brother, who is a member of the same firm

His brother, a member of the same firm

Trafalgar, which was Nelson's last battle

Trafalgar, Nelson's last battle

As positive statement is more concise than negative, and the active voice more concise than the passive, many of the examples given under Rules 11 and 12 illustrate this rule as well.

A common violation of conciseness is the presentation of a single complex idea, step by step, in a series of sentences which might to advantage be combined into one.

Macbeth was very ambitious. This led him to wish to become king of Scotland. The witches told him that this wish of his would come true. The king of Scotland at this time was Duncan.

Encouraged by his wife, Macbeth murdered Duncan. He was thus enabled to succeed Duncan as king. (55 words.)

Encouraged by his wife, Macbeth achieved his ambition and realized the prediction of the witches by murdering Duncan and becoming king of Scotland in his place. (26 words.)

14. Avoid a succession of loose sentences.

This rule refers especially to loose sentences of a particular type, those consisting of two co-ordinate clauses, the second introduced by a conjunction or relative. Although single sentences of this type may be unexceptionable (see under Rule 4), a series soon becomes monotonous and tedious.

An unskilful writer will sometimes construct a whole paragraph of sentences of this kind, using as connectives and, but, and less frequently, who, which, when, where, and while, these last in non-restrictive senses (see under Rule 3).

The third concert of the subscription series was given last evening, and a large audience was in attendance. Mr. Edward Appleton was the soloist, and the Boston Symphony Orchestra furnished the instrumental music. The former showed himself to be an artist of the first rank, while the latter proved Itself fully deserving of its high reputation. The interest aroused by the series has been very gratifying to the Committee, and it is planned to give a similar series annually hereafter. The fourth concert will be given on Tuesday, May 10, when an equally attractive program will be presented.

Apart from its triteness and emptiness, the paragraph above is bad because of the structure of its sentences, with their mechanical symmetry and sing-song. Contrast with them the sentences in the paragraphs quoted under Rule 10, or in any piece of good English prose, as the preface (Before the Curtain) to Vanity Fair.

If the writer finds that he has written a series of sentences of the type described, he should recast enough of them to remove the monotony, replacing them by simple sentences, by sentences of two clauses joined by a semicolon, by periodic sentences of two clauses, by sentences, loose or periodic, of three clauses—whichever best represent the real relations of the thought.

15. Express co-ordinate ideas in similar form.

This principle, that of parallel construction, requires that expressions of similar content and function should be outwardly similar. The likeness of form enables the reader to recognize more readily the likeness of content and function. Familiar instances from the Bible are the Ten Commandments, the Beatitudes, and the petitions of the Lord's Prayer.

The unskilful writer often violates this principle, from a mistaken belief that he should constantly vary the form of his expressions. It is true that in repeating a statement in order to emphasize it he may have need to vary its form. For illustration, see the paragraph from Stevenson quoted under Rule 10. But apart from this, he should follow the principle of parallel construction.

> Formerly, science was taught by the textbook method, while now the laboratory method is employed.

> Formerly, science was taught by the textbook method; now it is taught by the laboratory method.

The left-hand version gives the impression that the writer is undecided or timid; he seems unable or afraid to choose one form of expression and hold to it. The right-hand version shows that the writer has at least made his choice and abided by it.

By this principle, an article or a preposition applying to all the members of a series must either be used only before the first term or else be repeated before each term.

The French, the Italians, Spanish, and Portuguese	The French, the Italians, the Spanish, and the Portuguese

In spring, summer, or in winter	In spring, summer, or winter (In spring, in summer, or in winter)

Correlative expressions (both, and; not, but; not only, but also; either, or; first, second, third; and the like) should be followed by the same grammatical construction. Many violations of this rule can be corrected by rearranging the sentence.

It was both a long ceremony and very tedious.

The ceremony was both long and tedious.

A time not for words, but action

A time not for words, but for action

Either you must grant his request or incur his ill will.

You must either grant his request or incur his ill will.

My objections are, first, the injustice of the measure; second, that it is unconstitutional.

My objections are, first, that the measure is unjust; second, that it is unconstitutional.

See also the third example under Rule 12 and the last under Rule 13.

It may be asked, what if a writer needs to express a very large number of similar ideas, say twenty? Must he write twenty consecutive sentences of the same pattern? On closer examination he will probably find that the difficulty is imaginary, that his twenty ideas can be classified in groups, and that he need apply the principle only within each group. Otherwise he had best avoid the difficulty by putting his statements in the form of a table.

16. Keep related words together.

The position of the words in a sentence is the principal means of showing their relationship. The writer must therefore, so far as possible, bring together the words, and groups of words, that are related in thought, and keep apart those which are not so related.

The subject of a sentence and the principal verb should not, as a rule, be separated by a phrase or clause that can be transferred to the beginning.

> Wordsworth, in the fifth book of *The Excursion*, gives a minute description of this church.

> In the fifth book of *The Excursion*, Wordsworth gives a minute description of this church.

> Cast iron, when treated in a Bessemer converter, is changed into steel.

> By treatment in a Bessemer converter, cast iron is changed into steel.

The objection is that the interposed phrase or clause needlessly interrupts the natural order of the main clause. This objection, however, does not usually hold when the order is interrupted only by a relative clause or by an expression in apposition. Nor does it hold in periodic sentences in which the interruption is a deliberately used means of creating suspense (see examples under Rule 18).

The relative pronoun should come, as a rule, immediately after its antecedent.

There was a look in his eye that boded mischief.

In his eye was a look that boded mischief.

He wrote three articles about his adventures in Spain, which were published in *Harper's Magazine*.

He published in *Harper's Magazine* three articles about his adventures in Spain.

This is a portrait of Benjamin Harrison, grandson of William Henry Harrison, who became President in 1889.

This is a portrait of Benjamin Harrison, grandson of William Henry Harrison. He became President in 1889.

If the antecedent consists of a group of words, the relative comes at the end of the group, unless this would cause ambiguity.

The Superintendent of the Chicago Division, who

A proposal to amend the Sherman Act, which has been variously judged

A proposal, which has been variously judged, to amend the Sherman Act

A proposal to amend the much-debated Sherman Act

The grandson of William Henry Harrison, who

William Henry Harrison's grandson, Benjamin Harrison, who

A noun in apposition may come between antecedent and relative, because in such a combination no real ambiguity can arise,

> The Duke of York, his brother, who was regarded with hostility by the Whigs

Modifiers should come, if possible next to the word they modify. If several expressions modify the same word, they should be so arranged that no wrong relation is suggested.

> All the members were not present.

> Not all the members were present.

———————

> He only found two mistakes..

> He found only two mistakes.

———————

> Major R. E. Joyce will give a lecture on Tuesday evening in Bailey Hall, to which the public is invited, on "My Experiences in Mesopotamia" at eight P.M.
> On Tuesday evening at eight P. M., Major R. E. Joyce will give in Bailey Hall a lecture on "My Experiences in Mesopotamia." The public is invited.

17. In summaries, keep to one tense.

In summarizing the action of a drama, the writer should always use the present tense. In summarizing a poem, story, or novel, he should preferably use the present, though he may use the past if he prefers. If the summary is in the present tense, antecedent action should be expressed by the perfect; if in the past, by the past perfect.

> An unforeseen chance prevents Friar John from delivering Friar Lawrence's letter to Romeo. Juliet, meanwhile, owing to her father's arbitrary change of the day set for her wedding, has been compelled to drink the potion on Tuesday night, with the result

that Balthasar informs Romeo of her supposed death before Friar Lawrence learns of the nondelivery of the letter.

But whichever tense be used in the summary, a past tense in indirect discourse or in indirect question remains unchanged.

The Legate inquires who struck the blow.

Apart from the exceptions noted, whichever tense the writer chooses, he should use throughout. Shifting from one tense to the other gives the appearance of uncertainty and irresolution (compare Rule 15).

In presenting the statements or the thought of someone else, as in summarizing an essay or reporting a speech, the writer should avoid intercalating such expressions as "he said," "he stated," "the speaker added," "the speaker then went on to say," "the author also thinks," or the like. He should indicate clearly at the outset, once for all, that what follows is summary, and then waste no words in repeating the notification.

In notebooks, in newspapers, in handbooks of literature, summaries of one kind or another may be indispensable, and for children in primary schools it is a useful exercise to retell a story in their own words. But in the criticism or interpretation of literature the writer should be careful to avoid dropping into summary. He may find it necessary to devote one or two sentences to indicating the subject, or the opening situation, of the work he is discussing; he may cite numerous details to illustrate its qualities. But he should aim to write an orderly discussion supported by evidence, not a summary with occasional comment. Similarly, if the scope of his discussion includes a number of works, he will as a rule do better not to take them up singly in chronological order, but to aim from the beginning at establishing general conclusions.

18. Place the emphatic words of a sentence at the end.

The proper place for the word, or group of words, which the writer desires to make most prominent is usually the end of the sentence.

Humanity has hardly advanced in fortitude since that time, though it has advanced in many other ways.

Humanity, since that time, has advanced in many other ways, but it has hardly advanced in fortitude.

This steel is principally used for making razors, because of its hardness.

Because of its hardness, this steel is principally used in making razors.

The word or group of words entitled to this position of prominence is usually the logical predicate, that is, the new element in the sentence, as it is in the second example.

The effectiveness of the periodic sentence arises from the prominence which it gives to the main statement.

> Four centuries ago, Christopher Columbus, one of the Italian mariners whom the decline of their own republics had put at the service of the world and of adventure, seeking for Spain a westward passage to the Indies as a set-off against the achievements of Portuguese discoverers, lighted on America.

> With these hopes and in this belief I would urge you, laying aside all hindrance, thrusting away all private aims, to devote yourselves unswervingly and unflinchingly to the vigorous and successful prosecution of this war.

The other prominent position in the sentence is the beginning. Any element in the sentence, other than the subject, becomes emphatic when placed first.

> Deceit or treachery he could never forgive.

> So vast and rude, fretted by the action of nearly three thousand years, the fragments of this architecture may often seem, at first sight, like works of nature.

34 ‖ *William Strunk, Jr.*

A subject coming first in its sentence may be emphatic, but hardly by its position alone. In the sentence,

> Great kings worshipped at his shrine,

the emphasis upon kings arises largely from its meaning and from the context. To receive special emphasis, the subject of a sentence must take the position of the predicate.

> Through the middle of the valley flowed a winding stream.

The principle that the proper place for what is to be made most prominent is the end applies equally to the words of a sentence, to the sentences of a paragraph, and to the paragraphs of a composition.

IV.

A Few Matters of Form

Headings. Leave a blank line, or its equivalent in space, after the title or heading of a manuscript. On succeeding pages, if using ruled paper, begin on the first line.

Numerals. Do not spell out dates or other serial numbers. Write them in figures or in Roman notation, as may be appropriate.

August 9, 1918

Chapter XII

Rule 3

352d Infantry

Parentheses. A sentence containing an expression in parenthesis is punctuated, outside of the marks of parenthesis, exactly as if the expression in parenthesis were absent. The expression within is punctuated as if it stood by itself, except that the final stop is omitted unless it is a question mark or an exclamation point.

I went to his house yesterday (my third attempt to see him), but he had left town.

He declares (and why should we doubt his good faith?) that he is now certain of success.

(When a wholly detached expression or sentence is parenthesized, the final stop comes before the last mark of parenthesis.)

Quotations. Formal quotations, cited as documentary evidence, are introduced by a colon and enclosed in quotation marks.

The provision of the Constitution is:"No tax or duty shall be laid on articles exported from any state."

Quotations grammatically in apposition or the direct objects of verbs are preceded by a comma and enclosed in quotation marks.

I recall the maxim of La Rochefoucauld, "Gratitude is a lively sense of benefits to come."

Aristotle says, "Art is an imitation of nature."

Quotations of an entire line, or more, of verse, are begun on a fresh line and centred, but not enclosed in quotation marks.

Wordsworth's enthusiasm for the Revolution was at first unbounded:

Bliss was it in that dawn to be alive,

But to be young was very heaven!

Quotations introduced by that are regarded as in indirect discourse and not enclosed in quotation marks.

Keats declares that beauty is truth, truth beauty.

Proverbial expressions and familiar phrases of literary origin require no quotation marks.

These are the times that try men's souls.

He lives far from the madding crowd.

The same is true of colloquialisms and slang.

References. In scholarly work requiring exact references, abbreviate titles that occur frequently, giving the full forms in an alphabetical list at the end. As a general practice, give the references in parenthesis or in footnotes, not in the body of the sentence. Omit the words act, scene, line, book, volume, page, except when referring by only one of them. Punctuate as indicated below.

In the second scene of the third act

In III.ii (still better, simply insert III.ii in parenthesis at the proper place in the sentence)

After the killing of Polonius, Hamlet is placed under guard (IV. ii. 14).

———————

2 Samuel i:17-27

Othello II.iii 264-267, III.iii. 155-161

———————

Titles. For the titles of literary works, scholarly usage prefers italics with capitalized initials. The usage of editors and publishers varies, some using italics with capitalized initials, others using Roman with capitalized initials and with or without quotation marks. Use italics (indicated in manuscript by underscoring), except in writing for a periodical that follows a different practice. Omit initial A or The from titles when you place the possessive before them.

> The *Iliad*; the *Odyssey*; *As You Like It*; *To a Skylark*; *The Newcomes*; *A Tale of Two Cities*; Dicken's *Tale of Two Cities*.

V.

Words and Expressions Commonly Misused

(Many of the words and expressions here listed are not so much bad English as bad style, the commonplaces of careless writing. As illustrated under Feature, the proper correction is likely to be not the replacement of one word or set of words by another, but the replacement of vague generality by definite statement.)

All right. Idiomatic in familiar speech as a detached phrase in the sense, "Agreed," or "Go ahead." In other uses better avoided. Always written as two words.

As good or better than. Expressions of this type should be corrected by rearranging the sentence.

> My opinion is as good or better than his.

> My opinion is as good as his, or better (if not better).

As to whether. *Whether* is sufficient; see under Rule 13.

Bid. Takes the infinitive without to. The past tense is bade.

Case. The *Concise Oxford Dictionary* begins its definition of this word: "instance of a thing's occurring; usual state of affairs." In these two senses, the word is usually unnecessary.

> In many cases, the rooms were poorly ventilated.

> Many of the rooms were poorly ventilated.

> It has rarely been the case that any mistake has been made.

> Few mistakes have been made.

See Wood, *Suggestions to Authors*, pp. 68-71, and Quiller-Couch, *The Art of Writing*, pp. 103-106.

Certainly. Used indiscriminately by some speakers, much as others use very, to intensify any and every statement. A mannerism of this kind, bad in speech, is even worse in writing.

Character. Often simply redundant, used from a mere habit of wordiness.

> Acts of a hostile character
>
> Hostile acts

Claim, vb. With object-noun, means *lay claim to*. May be used with a dependent clause if this sense is clearly involved: "He claimed that he was the sole surviving heir." (But even here, "claimed to be" would be better.) Not to be used as a substitute for *declare*, *maintain*, or *charge*.

Compare. To *compare to* is to point out or imply resemblances, between objects regarded as essentially of different order; to *compare with* is mainly to point out differences, between objects regarded as essentially of the same order. Thus life has been compared to a pilgrimage, to a drama, to a battle; Congress may be compared with the British Parliament. Paris has been compared to ancient Athens; it may be compared with modern London.

Clever. This word has been greatly overused; it is best restricted to ingenuity displayed in small matters.

Consider. Not followed by *as* when it means, "believe to be." "I consider him thoroughly competent." Compare, "The lecturer considered Cromwell first as soldier and second as administrator," where "considered" means "examined" or "discussed."

Dependable. A needless substitute for *reliable, trustworthy*.

Due to. Incorrectly used for *through, because of,* or *owing to,* in adverbial phrases: "He lost the first game, due to carelessness." In correct use related as predicate or as modifier to a particular noun: "This invention is due to Edison;" "losses due to preventable fires."

Effect. As noun, means *result*; as verb, means *to bring about, accomplish* (not to be confused with *affect,* which means "to influence").

As noun, often loosely used in perfunctory writing about fashions, music, painting, and other arts: "an Oriental effect;" "effects in pale green;" "very delicate effects;" "broad effects;" "subtle effects;" "a charming effect was produced by." The writer who has a definite meaning to express will not take refuge in such vagueness.

Etc. Not to be used of persons. Equivalent to *and the rest, and so forth,* and hence not to be used if one of these would be insufficient, that is, if the reader would be left in doubt as to any important particulars. Least open to objection when it represents the last terms of a list already given in full, or immaterial words at the end of a quotation.

At the end of a list introduced by *such as, for example,* or any similar expression, *etc.* is incorrect.

Fact. Use this word only of matters of a kind capable of direct verification, not of matters of judgment. That a particular event happened on a given date, that lead melts at a certain temperature, are facts. But such conclusions as that Napoleon was the greatest of modern generals, or that the climate of California is delightful, however incontestable they may be, are not properly facts.

On the formula *the fact that,* see under Rule 13.

Factor. A hackneyed word; the expressions of which it forms part can usually be replaced by something more direct and idiomatic.

His superior training was the great factor in his winning the match.

He won the match by being better trained.

Heavy artillery is becoming an increasingly important factor in deciding battles.

Heavy artillery is playing a larger and larger part in deciding battles.

Feature. Another hackneyed word; like *factor* it usually adds nothing to the sentence in which it occurs.

> A feature of the entertainment especially worthy of mention was the singing of Miss A.

> (Better use the same number of words to tell what Miss A. sang, or if the programme has already been given, to tell something of how she sang.)

As a verb, in the advertising sense of *offer as a special attraction,* to be avoided.

Fix. Colloquial in America for *arrange, prepare, mend.* In writing restrict it to its literary senses, *fasten, make firm* or *immovable,* etc.

He is a man who. A common type of redundant expression; see Rule 13.

> He is a man who is very ambitious.

> He is very ambitious.

Spain is a country which I have always wanted to visit.

I have always wanted to visit Spain.

However. In the meaning *nevertheless*, not to come first in its sentence or clause.

> The roads were almost impassable. However, we at last succeeded in reaching camp.

> The roads were almost impassable. At last, however, we succeeded in reaching camp.

When *however* comes first, it means in whatever way or to whatever extent.

> However you advise him, he will probably do as he thinks best.

> However discouraging the prospect, he never lost heart.

Kind of. Not to be used as a substitute for *rather* (before adjectives and verbs), or except in familiar style, for *something like* (before nouns). Restrict it to its literal sense: "Amber is a kind of fossil resin;" "I dislike that kind of notoriety." The same holds true of *sort of*.

Less. Should not be misused for *fewer*.

> He had less men than in the previous campaign.

> He had fewer men than in the previous campaign.

Less refers to quantity, *fewer* to number. "His troubles are less than mine" means "His troubles are not so great as mine." "His troubles are fewer than mine" means "His troubles are not so numerous as mine." It is, however, correct to say, "The signers of the petition were less than a hundred, "where the round number, a hundred, is something like a collective noun, and less is thought of as meaning a less quantity or amount.

Line, along these lines. *Line* in the sense of *course of procedure, conduct, thought,* is allowable, but has been so much overworked, particularly in the phrase *along these lines,* that a writer who aims at freshness or originality had better discard it entirely.

Mr. B. also spoke along the same lines.

Mr. B. also spoke, to the same effect.

———————

He is studying along the line of French literature.

He is studying French literature.

Literal, literally. Often incorrectly used in support of exaggeration or violent metaphor.

———————

A literal flood of abuse

A flood of abuse

———————

Literally dead with fatigue

Almost dead with fatigue (dead tired)

———————

Lose out. Meant to be more emphatic than lose, but actually less so, because of its commonness. The same holds true of try out, win out, sign up, register up. With a number of verbs, out and up form idiomatic combinations: find out, run out, turn out, cheer up, dry up, make up, and others, each distinguishable in meaning from the simple verb. Lose out is not.

Most. Not to be used for *almost.*

> Most everybody
>
> Almost everybody

> Most all the time
>
> Almost all the time

Nature. Often simply redundant, used like *character.*

> Acts of a hostile nature
>
> Hostile acts

Often vaguely used in such expressions as "a lover of nature;" "poems about nature." Unless more specific statements follow, the reader cannot tell whether the poems have to do with natural scenery, rural life, the sunset, the untracked wilderness, or the habits of squirrels.

Near by. Adverbial phrase, not yet fully accepted as good English, though the analogy of *close by* and *hard by* seems to justify it. *Near*, or *near at hand*, is as good, if not better.

Not to be used as an adjective; use *neighboring.*

Oftentimes, ofttimes. Archaic forms, no longer in good use. The modern word is *often.*

One hundred and one. Retain the and in this and similar expressions, in accordance with the unvarying usage of English prose from Old English times.

One of the most. Avoid beginning essays or paragraphs with this formula, as, "One of the most interesting developments of modern science is, etc.;" "Switzerland is one of the most interesting countries of Europe." There is nothing wrong in this; it is simply threadbare and forcible-feeble.

People. *The people* is a political term, not to be confused with the *public.* From the people comes political support or opposition; from the public comes artistic appreciation or commercial patronage.

The word *people* is not to be used with words of number, in place of *persons.* If of "six people" five went away, how many "people" would be left?

Phase. Means a stage of transition or development: "the phases of the moon;" "the last phase." Not to be used for *aspect* or *topic.*

> Another phase of the subject

> Another point (another question)

Possess. Not to be used as a mere substitute for *have* or *own.*

> He possessed great courage.

> He had great courage (was very brave).

> ———

> He was the fortunate possessor of

> He owned

Respective, respectively. These words may usually be omitted with advantage.

> Works of fiction are listed under the names of their respective authors.

> Works of fiction are listed under the names of their authors.

> ———

> The one mile and two mile runs were won by Jones and Cummings respectively.

The one mile and two mile runs were won by Jones and by Cummings.

In some kinds of formal writing, as in geometrical proofs, it may be necessary to use *respectively*, but it should not appear in writing on ordinary subjects.

So. Avoid, in writing, the use of so as an intensifier: "so good;" "so warm;" "so delightful."

On the use of *so* to introduce clauses, see Rule 4.

Sort of. See under *Kind of.*

State. Not to be used as a mere substitute for say, remark. Restrict it to the sense of express fully or clearly, as, "He refused to state his objections."

Student body. A needless and awkward expression, meaning no more than the simple word *students*.

A member of the student body

A student

Popular with the student body

Liked by the students

The student body passed resolutions..

The students passed resolutions.

System. Frequently used without need.

Dayton has adopted the commission system of government.

Dayton has adopted government by commission.

———————

The dormitory system
Dormitories

Thanking you in advance. This sounds as if the writer meant, "It will not be worth my while to write to you again." Simply write, "Thanking you," and if the favor which you have requested is granted, write a letter of acknowledgment.

They. A common inaccuracy is the use of the plural pronoun when the antecedent is a distributive expression such as *each, each one, everybody, every one, many a man*, which, though implying more than one person, requires the pronoun to be in the singular. Similar to this, but with even less justification, is the use of the plural pronoun with the antecedent *anybody, anyone, somebody, someone*, the intention being either to avoid the awkward "he or she," or to avoid committing oneself to either. Some bashful speakers even say, "A friend of mine told me that they, etc."

Use *he* with all the above words, unless the antecedent is or must be feminine.

Very. Use this word sparingly. Where emphasis is necessary, use words strong in themselves.

Viewpoint. Write *point of view*, but do not misuse this, as many do, for view or opinion.

While. Avoid the indiscriminate use of this word for *and, but*, and *although*. Many writers use it frequently as a substitute for and or but, either from a mere desire to vary the connective, or from uncertainty which of the two connectives is the more appropriate. In this use it is best replaced by a semicolon.

> The office and salesrooms are on the ground floor, while the rest of the building is devoted to manufacturing.

> The office and salesrooms are on the ground floor; the rest of the building is devoted to manufacturing.

Its use as a virtual equivalent of although is allowable in sentences where this leads to no ambiguity or absurdity.

> While I admire his energy, I wish it were employed in a better cause.

This is entirely correct, as shown by the paraphrase,

> I admire his energy; at the same time I wish it were employed in a better cause.

Compare:

> While the temperature reaches 90 or 95 degrees in the daytime, the nights are often chilly.

> Although the temperature reaches 90 or 95 degrees in the daytime, the nights are often chilly.

The paraphrase,

> The temperature reaches 90 or 95 degrees in the daytime; at the same time the nights are often chilly,

shows why the use of while is incorrect.

In general, the writer will do well to use while only with strict literalness, in the sense of *during the time that.*

Whom. Often incorrectly used for *who* before *he said* or similar expressions, when it is really the subject of a following verb.

> His brother, whom he said would send him the money

> His brother, who he said would send him the money

The man whom he thought was his friend

The man who (that) he thought was his friend (whom he thought
his friend)

Worth while. Overworked as a term of vague approval and (with
not) of disapproval. Strictly applicable only to actions: "Is it
worth while to telegraph?"

> His books are not worth while.

> His books are not worth reading (not worth one's while to read;
> do not repay reading).

The use of *worth while* before a noun ("a worth while story")
is indefensible.

Would. A conditional statement in the first person requires *should*,
not *would*.

> I should not have succeeded without his help.

The equivalent of shall in indirect quotation after a verb in the
past tense is should, not would.

> He predicted that before long we should have a great surprise.

To express habitual or repeated action, the past tense, without
would, is usually sufficient, and from its brevity, more emphatic.

> Once a year he would visit the old mansion.

> Once a year he visited the old mansion.

VI.

Words Often Misspelled

accidentally
advice
affect
beginning
believe
benefit
challenge
criticize
deceive
definite
describe
despise
develop
disappoint
duel
ecstasy
effect
existence
fiery

formerly
humorous
hypocrisy
immediately
incidentally
latter
led
lose
marriage
mischief
murmur
necessary
occurred
parallel
Philip
playwright
preceding
prejudice
principal

privilege
pursue
repetition
rhyme
rhythm
ridiculous
sacrilegious
seize
separate
shepherd
siege
similar
simile
too
tragedy
tries
undoubtedly
until

Write today, tonight, tomorrow, and together without hyphens.
Write anyone, everyone, someone, sometime as one word.

THE END

Made in the USA
San Bernardino, CA
26 May 2015